Wild Wolf Encounters

TRUE STORIES OF WOLVES IN THE WILD

with pictures, poems, and links to videos

ISBN: 1468198033
ISBN 13: 9781468198034
Library of Congress Control Number: 2012900660
CreateSpace, North Charleston, South Carolina

to wolves
their friends and families

and to those who are learning
to live with them
in peace

Chapter Headings

Author's Prelude

My family and I travel to Yellowstone and Grand Teton National Parks two or three times a year, every year. Sometimes we are lucky enough to see wolves. Sometimes these are relatively close encounters.

Wolves are curious. They're curious about people. They take the time to stop and look before going on about their business. If a wolf takes the trouble to look you in the eyes, you will never forget it.

These stories are my first-hand observations. They happened. I was there and know they're true. The poems reflect my feelings about the encounter. The pictures and videos are ours. They were taken with equipment small enough to carry for miles into the backcountry and are therefore not of professional quality. That doesn't bother me, and I trust it won't bother you.

The purpose of this book, besides having fun and remembering some special times, is to share my personal experiences with wild wolves. My hope is that these stories can help to dispel fairy-tale notions of the "big bad wolf". The only myth-like truths about wolves are their size and beauty and the power they hold over the human psyche.

Please contact me through my blog: www.sweetplanetpoems.com, where you can also find more poems and pictures about wolves and other wild creatures, including humans. You may also want to visit my websites: www.wildwolfencounters.com and www.songsforabelovedfriend.com.

Videos can be accessed through the links provided; by going to YouTube, monicaglickman, and selecting the appropriate video; or by visiting www.wildwolfencounters.com.

Thank you!

Wolves Cross the Road

When we come to Yellowstone or the Grand Tetons, we like to spend several hours each day in the backcountry. As dwellers on the high, dry Western U.S. plateau, we particularly appreciate lakes and rivers, and travel to or along them as much as possible.

We carry binoculars, a small camera, and — usually — a video camera. Our equipment is not large or professional because it's already heavy enough. So is the water we need. Food is heavy and bulky, too, so we don't carry much of it and are always famished by day's end. Being famished plays a part in this story.

On our way to the trailhead, we pass a crowd standing along the road. Large groups usually mean something interesting is nearby, so we stop the car to see just what that could be. Wolves had killed an elk right by the road and were feeding there earlier. People await their return. We wait, too, for a while, and watch a juvenile bald eagle at the kill. Having miles to drive and hours to walk, we leave.

I'm sure the hike was beautiful, but that's not what I remember about the experience.

On the trip back, hungry and with an eye on the clock for our dinner reservation (miss it at your own risk), we see an even larger crowd. No wolves yet, but 150 people congregate. Should we join them? No, we decide reluctantly. Dinner is a high priority.

Driving on, and many miles later, I see something moving on the opposite embankment. In Yellowstone, one is never quite sure at first: is it a coyote, a bear, a deer, an elk — a wolf?! My body knows before my brain, because I can't speak — all I can do is point and gurgle. Not one wolf, but two. They let the car pass and cross behind us. We — and people in the car following — pull over, grab our cameras, and get out fast!

One of them, a black wolf, is already at the top of the road cut. His blue eyes offer a glowing contrast to dark fur. He looks at me for a moment and melts away into the forest. As I try to see more, others motion me along the road. There the second wolf has stopped to stare at my husband. Only a few feet away, his gaze is mild and curious. He lingers for a while and then is off about his business.

The picture is of him. The poems are inspired by these two. My guess is they were heading to the elk. The wolves were more willing to delay their dinner than we were.

LIKE A WHISPER

Wolves cross the road
and like a whisper
melt away
into thin air.

Black shadow
appears
like a thought
and a hope
and is gone.

WOLF DREAM

I remember when you came
to warm yourself by the fire,
and we lived in harmony.

Curious, you stop and stare.
A vague memory stirs.
Then survival dictates you flee

Black Wolf, White Wolf

One day in late May, on a visit to the Tetons, we decide to hike near the hotel, which has just opened for the season. The trail leads to one of our favorite lakes. In the past, we have seen moose with calves, coyote, beaver, trumpeter swans, ducks and geese, muskrat, and black bear at this lake. As more people travel to it, the chance of discovering something wild declines. But it's always wonderful to be there.

swans with cygnets

For the first half-mile, we notice coyote scat. After that, coyote scat gives way to something much larger. Still canine-like, but large. Some of it is white and decayed, but some looks fresh.

(Not everybody has pictures of scat in a book.)

Could wolves be so close to the hotel? Not possible! We pass more and more scat and wonder whether we will see an animal. We find bear prints and droppings, too, but only a few.

Here's a nice bear print. Can you see all five toes?

Then we see prints. Enormous prints! Enormous canine prints, deep and wide, not at all like coyote prints!

The body always knows before the brain. The brain is looking and figuring, deciding, evaluating. The body's physical response is immediate: this can be nothing other than a wolf print! The heart rate increases, the throat closes, language ability ceases. Something primal occurs, and it's not a fear response. It's a thrill that takes over the senses. I can't explain it, but I experience it every time I see a wolf or signs of one.

We keep walking, hoping but never expecting to see a wolf. We reach our destination, spend some time there relaxing, eating, and taking pictures, before deciding to head back.

Less than a mile from the lake, beside some willow bushes, the trail follows a slight depression. My husband, taller than I, stops and motions me to do so. He points — I look. A white wolf has come out of a willow into the open. She is just a few feet away. She looks at us and disappears into another bush. We try to breathe without moving. After a minute, a face materializes from a willow. Just the face, with eyes gazing out at us. A black face with startling eyes and beautiful ears. A collared face. The face contemplates us for several long seconds and withdraws.

We don't have a picture of this close encounter because we couldn't look anywhere but at that beautiful face. Quiet and still, we hope for more. My husband stomps around in the willows, but the wolves have vanished.

In another mile the path enters an open meadow. Something black is visible in the field. From the side, the legs and body are so long, I ask myself — what is that? A colt? What would a colt be doing here? A moose? Not thick enough for a moose. Oh, my God — it's the wolf!

The black wolf has circled around and is waiting for us in the meadow. Not close this time, at least a football field away, he begins to run perpendicular to us. Maintaining his distance, never advancing, he trots briskly back and forth, back and forth. Occasionally he disappears and then re-appears. Sometimes he pauses for a moment to face us. The running continues for some time, as we stand and watch. I can't take my eyes off him; luckily my husband has the camera out and is taking pictures.

The only time I am a bit scared is when he opens his mouth. The inside is bright red! I don't know if all black wolves have red mouths, but this one does. I ask my husband, "Why is he opening his mouth?" My husband is too busy filming and looking to answer this ridiculous question. I figure, and hope as well, that the wolf is opening his mouth because he has been dashing steadily from side to side and needs to breathe — that he is only panting.

And that certainly seems to be the case. Nothing in the wolf's stance, demeanor, or behavior indicates any threat or menace. He keeps his distance and never comes closer.

I have the distinct impression that the wolf is nervous and worried. There's an urgency to his rapid movements. The gait is not an easy, relaxed lope. We are in his territory, possibly the first humans to venture in after a long winter. The lodge has recently opened. What are humans doing here now? Perhaps we are near a den — it is the right time of year for pups — but I will never know.

Eventually the wolf runs back into the trees, the way he had come. At that point my husband takes the video camera from his pack and films a brief clip of the wolf facing us and then running away. We walk to the hotel, turning many times to look behind us into the forest. The wolf does not return.

We do return the next spring to find the trail closed.

We hear that wolves and bear frequent the area in elk calving season and notice their tracks close to the building

but do not take the trail to the lake. Next fall the trail is open, but we observe no tracks or animals. I sit in the sun near the willows and hope. The wolves have moved on.

You can see a short video of the black wolf running away on YouTube. You can decide for yourself if he looks threatening.

http://www.youtube.com/user/monicaglickman#p/a/u/0/LuJXmFwWCNs;
YouTube monicaglickman, Teton Wolf, 00:49; or www.wildwolfencounters.com/videos

POWER OF ATTRACTION

Intensely curious eyes
burn green gold
with interest bordering on fascination
as ancient comrades and hunting partners
struggle to remember
that which is beyond memory
but leaves its trace
in the powerful pull of mutual attraction.

MATING PAIR

Black wolf, white wolf
mating pair seeks strength in balance
no taboo keeps them apart

ONE MOMENT MORE

Look in my eyes
and take my measure
leave fear behind
a moment more
seeing you is weighty treasure
fleeting vision, lasting pleasure

a bluebird kind of day in the Tetons

MOUNTAIN BLUEBIRD

Where sky meets mountain
in tones of blue
shy songbird
cloaked impossibly in cerulean
flits to the yellow green willow

Wild Encounters in the Pelican Valley

This is a grizzly bear, wolf, buffalo, sandhill crane story. The wolf encounter wasn't particularly close, but it was melodious. The grizzly encounter was close, though.

Do grizzly bears have a sense of humor? I have heard and read many stories of grizzlies being tracked or hunted, who double back on their trackers. Hunter becomes the hunted. This is a mild version. Edward Abbey in *Down the River*, "Notes from a Cold River", tells a story about a boatman's previous grizzly experience while rafting the same Alaskan river. Hiking along the shore one day, he sees a bear in the water. The bear swims toward shore, and the man starts to run. When the bear reaches land, the man sprints even harder, pursued by the bear. The man races for his life, using every ounce of his strength. The bear, strangely enough, never narrows the gap between them, although he easily could. Bears can travel really fast, but that's another story, and this is a book about wolves. The fellow turns to look over his shoulder and sees on the bear's face an expression – of what – ferocity? No – of " 'noncommittal' curiosity"! The two run toward camp, still the same distance apart; the men in camp pull out their guns, and the bear veers off.

Curiosity coupled with a sense of humor? Can only humans possess these traits? Decide for yourself after reading this story.

One fall day in Yellowstone, we head to Pelican Valley. You can't hike there in the spring. In addition to being marshy with snowmelt, it's closed as prime grizzly bear habitat. This gives the grizzlies some freedom from human incursion after a long hibernation. Hungry, possibly cranky grizzlies and humans aren't a good mix.

A group of buffalo with calves runs near the trail. Could they be running from something? I have heard that animals may sometimes act especially lively and nimble when a wolf is nearby, as if to say, "Don't even bother; I'll be more trouble than benefit to you."

A mile down the trail, we meet two people coming from the opposite direction. They tell us there's a grizzly in the next drainage. We can see him if we leave the path and climb a small hill. We do, and the grizzly looks like a dark brown dot. Through binoculars we view him clearly. He's busy grubbing for food. We watch for a while and realize another grizzly wanders in the far hills.

Pelican Valley with grizzly dot

Then we hear a wolf howling — not close by. It's my husband who first notices. My husband, who can't always hear what I say to him from a foot away, can hear a wolf howling ten miles off. After some time the wolf appears, following the stream in the middle of the valley. He howls as he approaches. When he gets as close as he can without leaving the bank, he stops and looks at us, still howling. He makes his way downstream. When he disappears, sound and all, two sandhill cranes emerge from the bushes. A buffalo grazes in the distance, unperturbed by the wolf or the two grizzlies.

The first grizzly meanders along the broad valley and has now been out of sight for more than an hour. We watch the second as he climbs and vanishes into the distant hills. It's time to head back. We pack up and walk down the hill between us and the trail, wondering where the first grizzly went. Question answered. He's right here, behind us, on the trail! My, how that dark brown dot has grown!

We back off and to the side. The bear doesn't look up or at us or give any indication he knows or cares we are there. My husband films and we wait. Other hikers arrive, stopping at a respectful distance. Pretty soon there are people at three corners of a rectangle, with the bear in the middle. He sniffs and grubs along, taking his time, never looking up. I wonder if and which way we'll have to scatter. The bear continues to sniff, burrow, and mosey, eventually ambling off to the fourth corner of the rectangle and disappearing into the trees.

Does this bear have a sense of humor? The watchers become the watched. Was he curious about us? You decide.

That's one difference between bears and wolves. The bears I have seen often do not look at humans or acknowledge their existence, even when they are very close. Wolves always do.

To view the video, please visit http://www.youtube.com/watch?v=bVOiEcpuw0s or go to YouTube, monicaglickman, and select "grizzly, wolf, buffalo in Yellowstone's Pelican Valley", 8:06 minutes. You can also access the video at: www.wildwolfencounters.com/videos.

A few comments on the video:

Look for the buffalo rocks. I'm always seeing rocks that turn out not to be buffalo. These rocks are definitely buffalo.

Behind the wind noise in the wolf segment, you can hear a faint howl. The howl was much more prevalent in person. You can also get a glimpse of the second grizzly in the distance in the wolf segment.

The grizzly you see far down the valley is the same one you see in close-up later in the video. Go in peace, preferably in the other direction, Mr. Grizzly!

Note the hump on the grizzly and how he does not look at or acknowledge us — very unlike the wolf, who looks as he howls. And what about that tush?! It reminds me of something...

PRINTS IN THE MUD

Bigfoot precedes me
down the trail,
five large toes
with claws for nails.

Round furry tush
like my dog's behind,
mind your business
and I'll mind mine.

Here are some related pictures. The poem was written about a different grizzly behind, but you get the idea.

And another:

Hello and Good-Bye at Shoshone Lake

Shoshone Lake in Yellowstone National Park is one of my favorite spots on earth. We hike there every time we go, unless the snow in late spring is still too deep. There are several routes leading to Shoshone, and often we will take more than one on a visit to the park.

On our last fall trip we did just that, hiking to Shoshone on the DeLacy Creek trail and then again, on another day, via Lewis Lake and the Lewis River. Both are gorgeous places to explore.

The DeLacy Creek trail follows a meadow to the lake. We always look for animals as we walk but have never seen any before this last trip. We get just a glimpse this time.

You can see the lake from various points along the trail, gleaming in the sun or cloaked in clouds or even snow, depending upon the season. Shoshone Lake is beautiful in any light and any weather.

But the sun is shining today, and there are lots of people on the trail – more than usual for some reason, and all coming out. No one is at the lake when we arrive. We eat lunch and watch the water. It's very quiet with no wind.

My husband decides to take a nap, while I walk around the lake for a bit. I love walking along Shoshone Lake between the DeLacy Creek trail and Lewis Lake, but going all the way out in that direction requires a very early start and a drop-off, with the car at one end and two people meeting in the middle, one re-tracing his steps.

There is no time for that today. I step past bear droppings filled with the residue of nearby raspberry bushes. When I return an hour or so later, my husband is still asleep. We pack up to go. As we leave the lakeside, we notice a large pile of canine scat – way too big for coyote – at the trailhead. We could not have missed stumbling over this scat on the way in. A large, black canine (also not coyote) is just disappearing into the tall grasses across the meadow. A raven flies directly over my head. I hear the sound his wings make beating the air. Ravens and wolves share a tie that binds, not well understood by humans.

The wolf must have come to the lake, seen my husband asleep on the ground, left his calling card, and disappeared. End of story. No snarling, baring of teeth, menacing behavior, or death at the lake to report. And no pictures of this wolf, either. I should have taken a picture of the calling card but didn't!

SHOSHONE LAKE

Shine on, Shoshone Lake,
sparkle in the sun
glitter in cool blue beauty
dream of frogs croaking
in the moist meadow
as you kindle a calm spark within.

PERFECT ANGLE

My Shoshone
perfect from every angle
heaven in every season –
the mind trails along your shore

The Black Wolf with the Blue Face

Wolf Lake

It was no accident that we happened upon this wolf. The day before we had hiked to – of all places – Wolf Lake in Yellowstone. There is more than one route to Wolf Lake. One passes by Grebe Lake; the other, the way we came, begins at Ice Lake.

Wolf Lake is a place of utter serenity. We never see anyone there. This time swans and cygnets drift with the currents at the far end of the lake. Bluebirds flit back and forth between the trees at the forest edge. The lake empties into the Gibbon River, here a quiet, shallow stream, which one must ford to go onward. But I am getting ahead of myself.

The trail to Grebe Lake is across the Gibbon River.

We still have a mile to go before we reach Wolf Lake. Two people approach with backpacks on. We greet them, and they stop us. They have an interesting story to tell. While they were camping the night before at Grebe Lake, two miles beyond Wolf, predators had killed an elk just a few feet from their tent. Whether wolves or bear had made the kill, they didn't know until the next morning. The dying elk was not quiet, nor were other elk in the herd. The couple got no sleep that night and couldn't wait to make a beeline out of the backcountry. A black wolf walked by their campsite as they packed up the next morning. They think he took their tent cover during the night. For some reason they felt safer walking out in the opposite direction from their car, even though the trip is much longer that way. They said they were very glad to see humans!

And meeting them is lucky for us. We look at each other. Grebe Lake today? That would be a production. Too late in the day to stop for more than a few minutes at either Wolf or Grebe Lake, we would come out miles from our car and have to hitchhike back to it at dusk. Not such a great idea. However, tomorrow brings a new opportunity.

Over breakfast the next day we discuss and reject various options. There's only one place we want to be. The Grebe Lake trailhead is an hour's drive, and there is a very good chance the trail will be closed — assuming the backpackers had told a ranger about their experience. We reach an agreement to honor any sign closing the trail.

Off we head, one of us not so sure the other can be relied upon to keep that agreement. No worries. We get there — no sign. Evidently the couple had kept their adventure to themselves.

Since grizzly and black bears don't need to read about a kill in the vicinity, we proceed cautiously. Well, since this is a true story, I must say that one of us proceeds cautiously; the other simply proceeds. We see no bears or other animals en route. We reach Grebe Lake and take a quick look around. No wolves, no tracks — oh — but three humans. Two are fishing and tell us that, just an hour earlier, three wolves had been busy with something on the other side of the lake. We have a pretty good idea what that something is. Three wolves — three different colors: one black, one grey, and one white. The white wolf had run off by himself into the woods. Eventually the other two disappeared as well. Hikers had passed without stopping or noticing anything unusual.

I think — darn — we missed wolves by an hour. My next thought is — wait — there's a kill. They'll be back!

A third person reads on a rock while her friends fish. She looks up and says she feels quite nervous that a wolf might appear. Nervous? O.K. Perhaps he will carry off her book.

We continue on the trail around to the other side of the lake. As we approach, ravens begin to call and scream. They fly to and from a tree near the water. They carry on incessantly, making a deep clicking thump in their throats. I don't know what this thump is called or if it has a name. But it sounds like they are trying to crack a coconut inside closed mouths. They whirr and wheel overhead, continuing to make a big commotion.

A strange single sound comes from the nearby forest – not a howl or any sound I have ever heard before. More like a bark than anything else. Only one. It could be a tree branch rubbing or ratcheting, but there isn't enough wind. There isn't any wind.

Something interesting could be about to happen. I am going to be patient and let it.

I find a spot a short distance from the lake, near the raven tree and screened by small aspen. I get out my lunch and ready the camera, video, and binoculars. If they're not ready to use, I won't be able to look away to find them. I sit down and make myself comfortable. I eat; I wait. My husband has been wandering around, looking for the kill. He returns and joins me. We both wait. We don't have to wait for too long.

After about an hour, the black wolf emerges from the forest, walks into the meadow, and lies down in the shade of a tree. His face is blue – like a blue merle dog. The ravens quiet immediately. The wolf sits but doesn't really rest. His ears twitch, his head moves back and forth. He looks in every direction. Is he expecting company? He lays his head down; in a second he picks it up again. This must be the way a wolf in the wild gets to relax. He stays for quite a while.

We take pictures and videos and watch through the binoculars. He gets up and returns to the forest.

Well, that was awesome! What now? What else? We'll wait some more. We move our things a little closer to the lake. Still screened by small bushes, we have a good view of the nearby meadow, forest, and lakeshore. A coyote peers from trees near the wolf's resting place. The animal looks wistful but does not approach. He cannot contend with a wolf for food. Eagles soar overhead, diving low into the trees, their strange calls echoing. Binoculars and cameras are ready for action. We are not disappointed.

Perhaps a half-hour later, the wolf enters the meadow from a closer part of the forest. I see him emerge from the shadows at the forest edge, just as I have always imagined a wolf would appear. He looks around, walks slowly to the lakeshore, and goes to his kill.

The kill is right by the water, hidden in the tall grasses by the side of the lake. We watch him at the kill for a very long while. I'm struck by how delicately he eats – a small bit at a time, chewing each mouthful carefully, often wiping his mouth with his tongue. Not the tearing and rending I would have assumed.

But this is still not a relaxing meal. Wary and alert, looking around constantly, stopping to listen, the wolf comes and goes, leaving the kill and moving up into the meadow. People approach on the trail, and he retreats into the forest. They pass without slowing down, although they look back as they walk. When they are out of sight, the wolf re-enters the meadow. He continues to eat, with many interruptions to stop, look, listen, and circle. We wait until he returns to the shadows for what seems like the final time.

It's getting late. We have several miles to hike before we reach the car, and dinner is important to us, too. We pack up and leave. A raven flies a few feet over my head. I hear the sound of his wings moving the air. The trail takes us by the water. Now we know where to look for the kill. My husband takes a picture. I tell him I plan to delete it when we get home. I see the photo a few weeks later on the computer; strangely beautiful in the evening light, it takes a few moments to realize what it is.

We continue to the place we saw the fishermen. There the trail leaves the lake and enters the forest. As we turn to look, the wolf has once again returned to the meadow and is making his way to the kill. Dinner is a powerful pull, because it's very hard to leave.

Did he know we were watching him? Almost certainly. On the videos and in the pictures, he looks directly at us.

I sneezed once. And I believe the ravens were warning him about us. Red alert! Humans approaching! Humans hiding! And, of course, we must smell like humans to a wolf.

You can see four videos of the black wolf with the blue face on YouTube:
http://www.youtube.com/user/monicaglickman#p/u/4/D03L8OG5kSQ
http://www.youtube.com/user/monicaglickman#p/u/3/9tPT3ym4UOU
http://www.youtube.com/user/monicaglickman#p/u/1/d9kMmEiKdRs
http://www.youtube.com/user/monicaglickman#p/a/u/2/63aMvSnShIE

You can also visit YouTube, monicaglickman, and select Black Wolf with the Blue Face, 1:04 minutes; Black Wolf with the Blue Face at his Kill, 4:47; Eagles soar, ravens call, wolf watches at Grebe Lake, 2:53; and Wolf at Grebe Lake, Yellowstone National Park, 3:26

or find links to these four videos at www.wildwolfencounters.com/videos

GREBE LAKE

Happy am I
called Grebe Lake
reflecting passing clouds
and the hills that surround me
home to many creatures
happy am I

Happy am I
the black wolf with the blue face
rests beside me
breathing deeply of my cool stillness
I will be calm and quiet
and show him my best welcome

Happy am I

MANNERS

The black wolf with the blue face
dines with reserve
wiping his mouth carefully
with his tongue
taking time to savor the flavor
nervously watching
for unwelcome company
but retiring graciously
at frequent intervals
so the humans,
should they desire,
can share his splendid feast

THE COMING

Black shadow at the forest edge
grows and deepens
darkens to a thicker ink
begins to quiver
moving now into the meadow
a black wolf emerges
from my imagination

LAST LIGHT

Last summer's light
bathes the forest
in the soft glow of evening
setting season lingers
its easy ways
packed and ready
for the long journey south

FOREST CHATTER

Tree branches rub
and ratchet in the wind
chatter like a flock of exotic birds
moan of deeply-rooted places
rustle their secrets

THE GOING

Rested, satisfied
returning to the shadows
satiating dreams

WOLF LAKE

Sublime quiet
heightened by birdsong
wind's caress
wolf's howl
coyote's yip
water's lap
heart's beat

Wild Harmony

It's fitting to close the book with this story, because the day marked the end of one of our visits to Yellowstone. It was also our first near encounter with a wild wolf.

Unlike our usual late start, after a run for my husband and yoga for me, followed by a big breakfast (very important) and a drive to the trailhead, this time is different. We are checking out of Lake Hotel and driving to the Tetons. It's a short trip, and the plan is to get an early start on the trail to the lake described in "Black Wolf, White Wolf". Our chances of seeing wildlife at the lake increase that way.

We didn't get to the trail early, but we did see, and especially hear, wildlife en route.

The road follows Lake Yellowstone, beautiful in the early morning light. West Thumb Geyser Basin steams sulphur smells into the air; its iridescent pools gleam with rainbow colors. But that's another story, too – or poem – and we don't stop there today. Turning south on the road heading directly to the Tetons, we pass an elk on the side grazing. Another bugles, that impossibly high-pitched fall mating call. We drive several miles and see – something – large and completely white cross the road from right to left a few car lengths ahead. Big and tall enough to be a bear but slim, not bulky; the legs are so long, it takes a moment to register – wolf! The wolf looks at us as it crosses and disappears into the trees. We stop the car and get out but can see nothing.

However, what we can do is hear. From the forest on the right side of the road, from where the white wolf has come, a howl begins. The deep, low, mournful sound, almost other-worldly, rises and falls, singing a message that communicates sorrow and loss. As the howl continues, an elk begins to bugle. The two creatures, neither visible but not far apart, raise their voices in wild harmony inscrutable to humans.

The howling continues for more than an hour. We try to follow the sound; while not moving, it never seems to get closer. Since this is our first encounter with a wolf, I wonder what would happen should we actually stumble upon the howler. We make no progress and finally give up the attempt. I wish I had started howling myself but never thought of it.

To hear the wolf howl/elk bugle duet, please visit www.wildwolfencounters.com/videos

or http://www.youtube.com/user/monicaglickman#p/u/7/DooNC4XpMpI

You can also go to YouTube and select "early morning call of the wild from Yellowstone National Park" 1:23.

.

Recapitulation

A few words about the prose and poetry. When I began to write in a creative way, I wrote poetry. That's what emerged. I still write poetry and find I can rely on it to pack a big wallop into a short space. I prefer succinct to drawn-out. I ascribe this to my legal training, although this may come as a shock to some.

But when it came time to share some things about wolves, I felt I needed to use prose to tell the story. Prose is accessible to more people, and one can say that it is more objectively true. I can say that about these stories. I was there; I saw; I wrote down. That is also so for the poems – I was there, I wrote. But the poems contain something other than objective truth. They reflect – and accurately – the truth of my heart.

When, for example, I finished "Power of Attraction" and the base of my spine tingled, I knew the poem communicated what I saw and felt, what I needed to say about the experience. Objective or not, the poems are my truth. Hurray for poetry!

MY BROTHER THE WOLF*

My brother the wolf
sings his music under clear stars
a chant I recognize but cannot name
haunts me

My brother the wolf
hears the fear and longing
in our hearts
sees confusion at a glance

My brother the wolf,
no prodigal child,
will not be tamed,
clings with ferocity to ways wild

My brother the wolf
lies quietly at a distance
waiting patiently for me to acknowledge
our ancient ties

*....my brother the wolf, my sister the sea...
my lover the moon....
John Denver

Thanks

*to my husband
for your good-natured patience over the years
as city girl transformed
into lover of wilderness*

*Without you, I might have rushed through Yellowstone
or never have found it at all*